Phonics Vowels

Written by Lillian Duggan

Illustrations by Maribel Suarez

FlashKids

An imprint of Sterling Children's Books

This book belongs to

_____

FLASH KIDS, STERLING, and the distinctive Sterling logo are registered trademarks of
Sterling Publishing Co., Inc.

Published by Sterling Publishing Co., Inc.
387 Park Avenue South, New York, NY 10016
Text and illustrations © 2006 by Flash Kids
Distributed in Canada by Sterling Publishing
c/o Canadian Manda Group, 165 Dufferin Street
Toronto, Ontario, Canada M6K 3H6
Distributed in the United Kingdom by GMC Distribution Services
Castle Place, 166 High Street, Lewes, East Sussex, England BN7 1XU
Distributed in Australia by Capricorn Link (Australia) Pty. Ltd.
P.O. Box 704, Windsor, NSW 2756, Australia

Sterling ISBN 978-1-4114-3445-5

Manufactured in China

Lot #:
2 4 6 8 10 9 7 5 3
10/10

For information about custom editions, special sales, premium and
corporate purchases, please contact Sterling Special Sales
Department at 800-805-5489 or specialsales@sterlingpublishing.com.

Cover design and production by Mada Design, Inc.

Dear Parent,

Learning vowel sounds is an important part of reading. This book will help your child identify short and long vowel sounds. This book includes matching activities, mazes, hidden pictures, story activities, and lots of practice distinguishing the different vowel sounds. To get the most from the activities included in this book, follow these simple steps:

- Find a comfortable place where you and your child can work quietly together.
- Encourage your child to go at his or her own pace.
- Help your child sound out the letters and identify the pictures.
- Offer lots of praise and support.
- Let your child reward his or her work with the included stickers.
- Most of all, remember that learning should be fun! Take time to look at the pictures, laugh at the funny characters, and enjoy this special time spent together.

Take That Hat off That Cat!

The sound you hear in the middle of h<u>a</u>t and c<u>a</u>t is the short **a** sound.

Circle the things that have the short **a** sound.

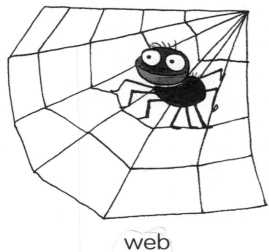

web

can

bat

boy

Help the Bat Find the Ants

The bat is hungry. Draw a path from the bat to the ants.

Follow the things that have the short **a** sound.

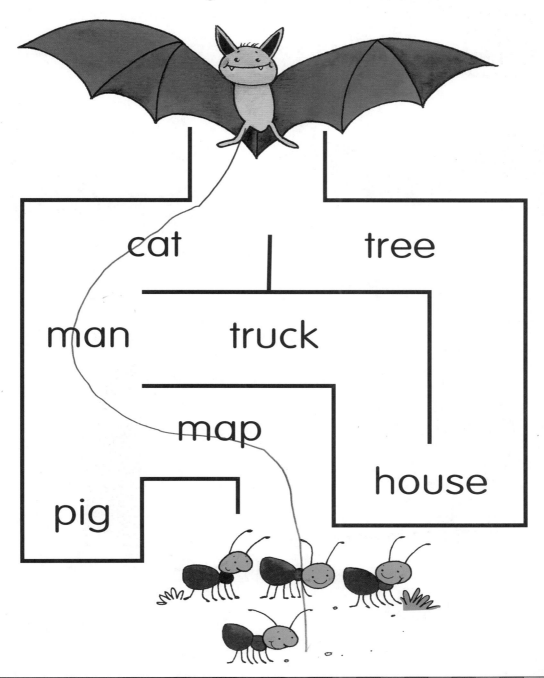

cat

tree

man

truck

map

house

pig

Rhyming Rams

Read the word that goes with the picture.

Write the rhyming word.

bat

cat

fan

man

Short a Picnic

Circle the short **a** words you see in the picture.

(cat) ram ham fan sand

Shhhhhh! The Hens Are in Bed!

The sound you hear in the middle of h<u>e</u>n and b<u>e</u>d is the short **e** sound. Circle the pictures that have the short **e** sound.

rug

desk

dog

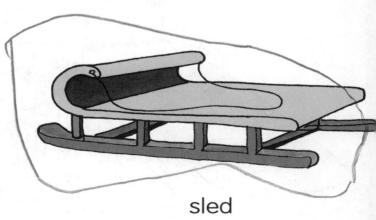

sled

8

My Pet Spider's Web

Ben's spider wants to fill his web with short **e** sound words.

Circle the things he wants.

bed   pen   web   bell   desk

Rhyme Time with Ben and Glen

Read the word that goes with the picture.

Write the rhyming word.

net

jerplaen

vest

nest

The Hen or the Men?

Look at the pictures. Answer each question with **hen** or **men**.

hen

men

Who wears vests?

man

Who sits in a nest?

hen

Who is wet?

hen

Who was in a jet?

men

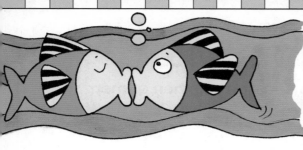

Fish Lips Give the Best Kisses

The sound you hear in the middle of f<u>i</u>sh, l<u>i</u>ps, and k<u>i</u>ss is the short **i** sound. Circle the pictures that have the short **i** sound.

crib

bat

sun

pig

Silly Pig!

Jig the pig likes only things that have the short **i** sound.

Circle the things Jig likes.

mitt   fish   brick

Win-a-Pin
Rhyming Contest

Read the word that goes with the picture.

Write the rhyming word.

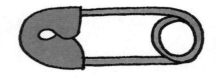

fin

Pin

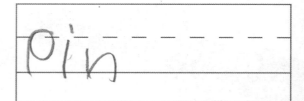

dish

Fish

The Story of the Six Pigs

Look at the picture. Fill in the missing words.

(kiss) (wigs) (pig) (dig)

Six pigs wearing **Wigs**

went to **dig** on a hill.

One pig got a **Kiss**

from a **pig** named Bill.

Fox-y Socks

The sound you hear in the middle of f<u>o</u>x and s<u>o</u>ck is the short **o** sound. Circle the pictures that have the short **o** sound.

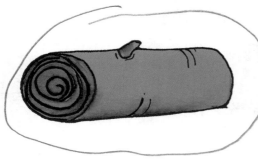

log

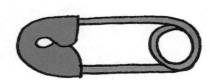

pin

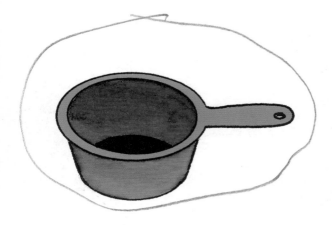

pot

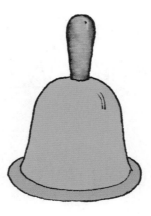

bell

Molly's Jog

Molly is jogging around the pond.

Circle the things with the short **o** sound that she will see.

ox fox rock log pond dog

Pog the Rhyming Dog

Read the word that goes with the picture.

Write the rhyming word.

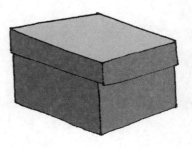

stop

moe

fox

BO 5

Goodnight
Ox, Fox, Dog, and Hog

Look at the picture. Read the story.

Draw a line from each word in the box to its picture.

ox   box   fox   log   hog   cot

The ox sleeps on top of the box. So does the fox.

The dog sleeps in the log. What about the hog?

He must sleep on the cot.

Gummy Bugs

The sound you hear in the middle of g<u>u</u>m and b<u>u</u>g is the short **u** sound. Circle the pictures that have the short **u** sound.

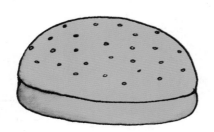

bun

doll

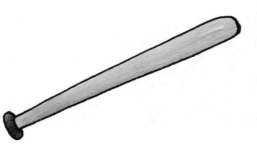

bat

truck

Dudley Duck Drives a Truck

Help Dudley Duck get to the sun.
Follow the short **u** sound
words to help him.

bun

nest

pig

win

vest

fun

hen

tub

pin

lip

men

run

pup

bun

The Snug Bug Rhymers

Read the word that goes with the picture. Write the rhyming word.

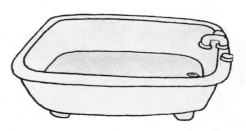

cub

gum

Bugs Going Nuts

Look at the picture. Finish the sentences with the words in the box.

bus   nuts   bugs   sun

The _____ are in line

in the hot _____ .

They will get on the _____

to go buy _____ .

Find Short o
and Short a, Okay?

Color the short **a** words orange. Color the short **o** words brown.

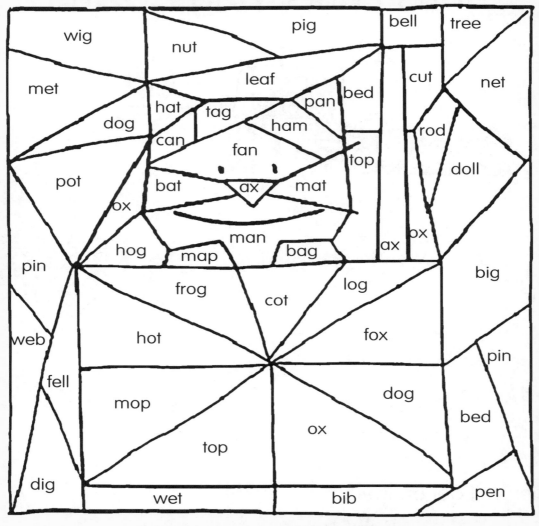

Fill in the words to finish the sentence.

The _____ is in the _____ .

Give Me an a?

Say the words the pictures show. Write the letter to finish each word.

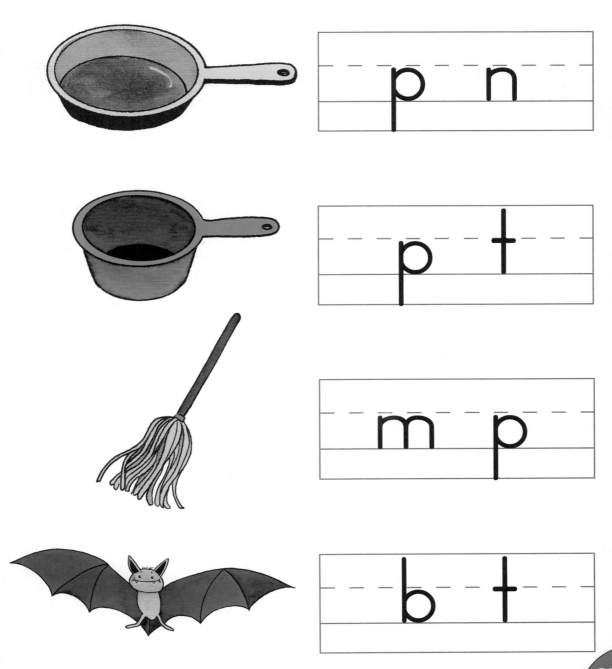

p _ n

p _ t

m _ p

b _ t

Hey, Short e!

Color the short **e** words blue. Color the short **i** words pink.
Color the short **o** words yellow.

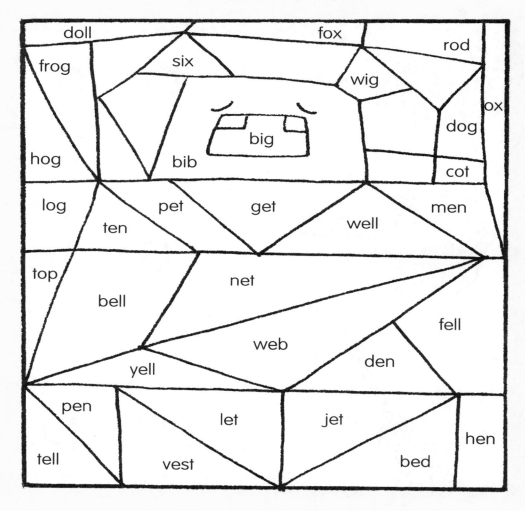

Fill in the words to finish the sentence.

The _____ is in the _____.

Can I Buy a Short i?

Say the words the pictures show. Write the letter to finish each word.

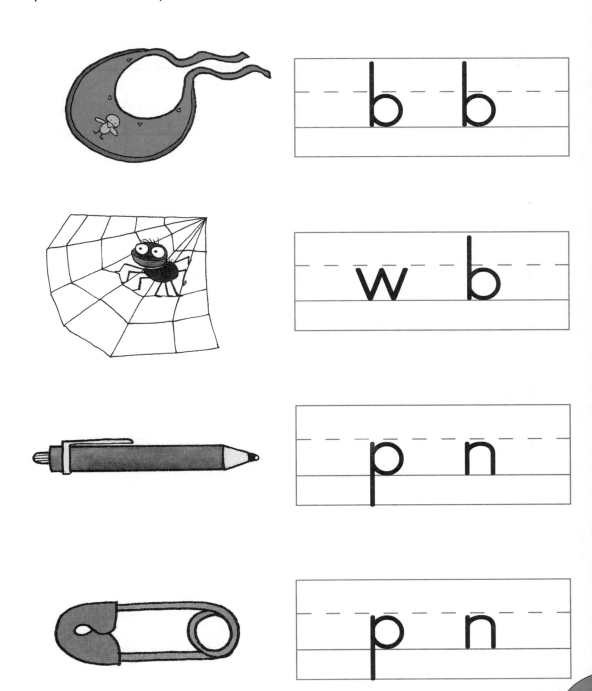

b b

w b

p n

p n

I'm Looking for u!

Color the short **u** words red.

Color the short **a** words brown.

Color the short **e** words blue.

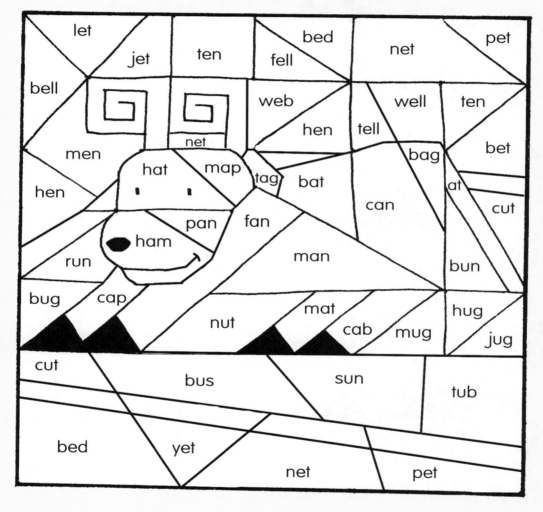

The [_____] is on the [_____].

Short Vowels All Around

Say the words the pictures show. Write the letter to finish each word.

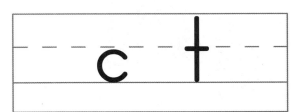
c t

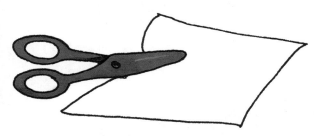

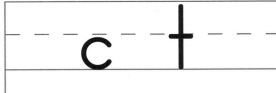
c t

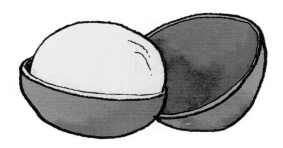

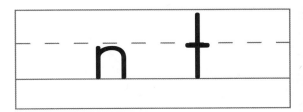
n t

n t

Jake Loves Cake!

When a says its name, it is long **a**.

You hear the long **a** sound in **Jake** and **cake**.

Circle the pictures that have the long **a** sound.

tail

vase

bat

rake

pan

Your Cap and Your Cape, Sir?

Add **e** to the end of these words
to make the long **a** sound.

can

tap

Sal Has Set Sail

When **a** is followed by **i** in a word,
a makes a long **a** sound, and **i** is silent.

Draw a line from each word to the picture it names.

bait

bat

pal

pail

Mr. Gail, the Rhyming Mailman

Read the word that goes with the picture.

Write the rhyming word.

The mail does not fail, ma'am.

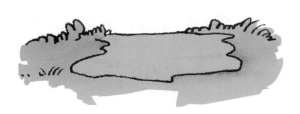

lake

train

The Story of Blake

Read the story. Fill in the blanks with long **a** words.

Blake set sail on a lake.

A man in a cape
helped Blake.

Blake baked
the man a cake.

Blake sailed on the _____ .

The man wore a _____ .

Blake and the man will eat _____ .

The Queen of Big Feet

You hear the long **e** sound in **queen** and **feet**.

Circle the pictures that have the long **e** sound.

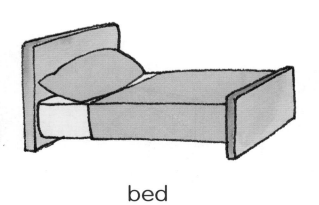

key

beads

bed

leaf

Mel Loves a Big Meal!

When **e** is followed by another **e** or an **a**
in a word, **e** makes a long **e** sound,
and the other vowel is silent.

Draw a line from each word to the picture it names.

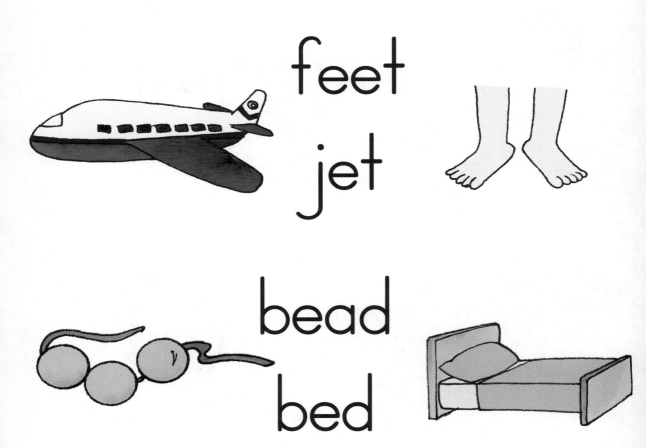

feet

jet

bead

bed

These Seals Rhyme for Their Meals

Read the word that goes with the picture. Write the rhyming word.

beet

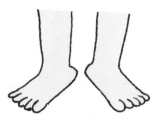

tree

What a Sweet Queen!

Look at the picture. Read the story. Draw a line from each word to its picture.

seal   peas   queen   beets   deer

The queen said, "Let them eat peas and beets."

The seal and deer were happy.

Five Nice Mice

You hear the long **i** sound in **five**, **nice**, and **mice**.

Circle the pictures that have the long **i** sound.

tie

bike

pig

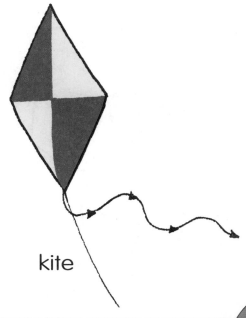

kite

Tim Is Never on Time

Add **e** to the end of these words to make the long **i** sound.

pin

kit

Mike and Ike
Like to Rhyme

Read the word that goes with the first picture.

Write the rhyming word under the second picture.

hike

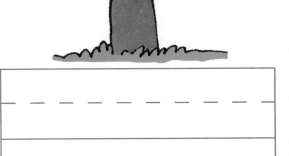

ride

The Hiking Nine

Read the story. Fill in the blanks below with long **i** words.

Nine girls
were on a hike.
They had a kite.
It flew over the pines.

There were _____ girls.

They went on a _____ .

They flew a _____ .

It went over the _____ .

Let's Soap Up the Goat!

You hear the long **o** sound in **soap** and **goat**. Circle the pictures that have the long **o** sound.

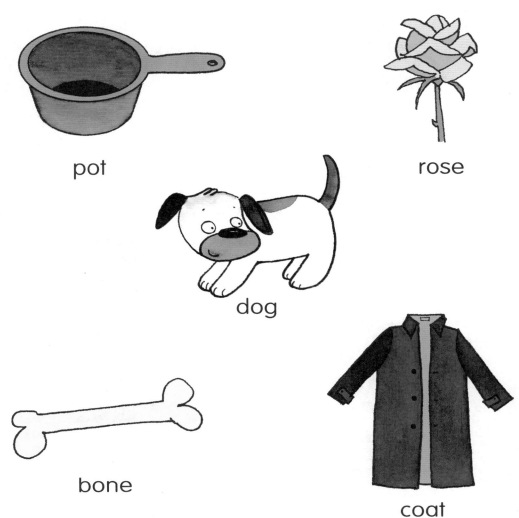

pot

rose

dog

bone

coat

Please! Not Another Note!

Add **e** to the end of these words
to make the long **o** sound.

mop

tot

Great Goal, Toad!

When **o** is followed by **a** in a word, **o** makes a long **o** sound, and the other vowel is silent.

Draw a line from each word to the picture it names.

coat

cot

bat

boat

Rhyming Goat on a Boat

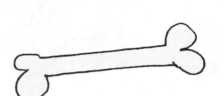

Read the word that goes with the picture. Write the rhyming word.

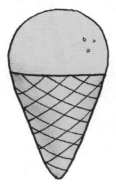

cone

road

Ode to Long O

Look at the picture. Read the story.

Draw a line from each word in the box to its picture.

toad   nose   note   rose   road

This note smells like a rose.

I smell it with my nose.

"Who wrote the note?"

asked the toad on the road.

Mules Rule!

You hear the long **u** sound in **mule** and **rule**.
Circle the pictures that have the long **u** sound.

flute

drum

fruit

suit

rug

One Cute Dude!

Fill in each sentence with a word from the box.

cut   cute   tub   tube

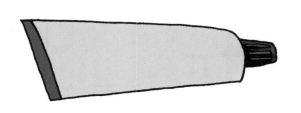

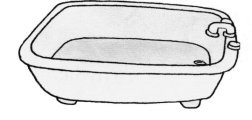

This is a

_____

This is a

_____

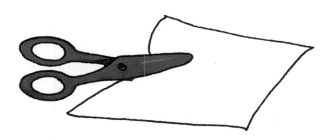

These can

_____

He is

_____

Silly Fruit in a Suit

When **u** is followed by **i** in a word, **u** makes a long **u** sound, and **i** is silent. Finish each sentence with a word to match the picture.

Amy likes to eat **fr**_____.

Harry got a new **s**_____.

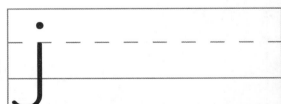

I like to drink **j**_____.

Luke and Duke's World of Rhymes

Put an X over the word in each row
that does not rhyme.

cube

tub

tube

fan

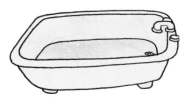

June

Jan

sit

suit

fruit

Can a and e Get Along?

Color the long **a** words light blue. Color the long **e** words brown.
Color the long **i** words dark blue.

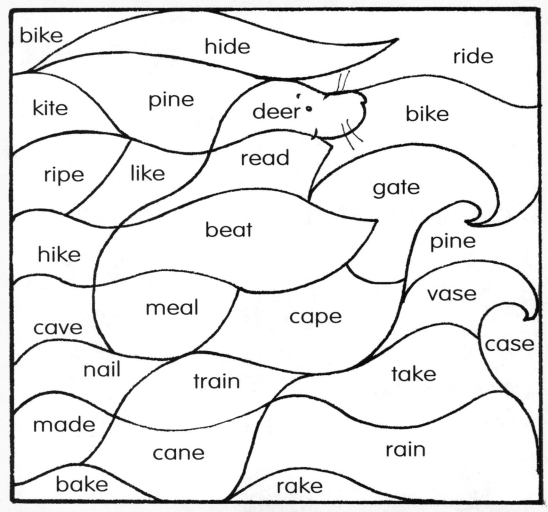

Fill in the words to finish the sentence.

The [_____] is riding a [_____].

I Long for a and e

Say the word the picture shows.

Write the missing letters to finish the word.

 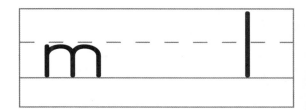

m _ _ l

 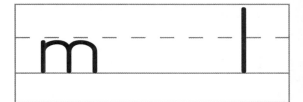

m _ _ l

 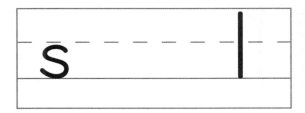

s _ _ l

 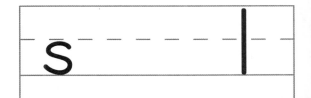

s _ _ l

Row Away with Long a

Color the long **a** words green. Color the long **o** words yellow.
Color the long **e** words blue.

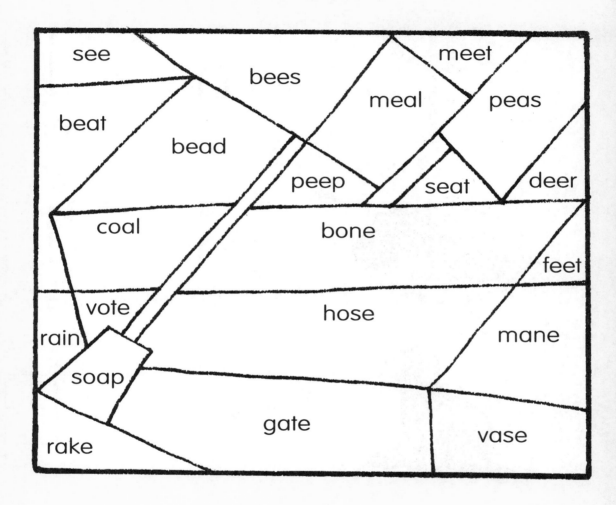

see

meet

bees

meal

peas

beat

bead

peep

seat

deer

coal

bone

feet

vote

hose

rain

mane

soap

rake

gate

vase

Fill in the words to finish the sentence.

The ⬚ is on the ⬚ .

O My, It's Long 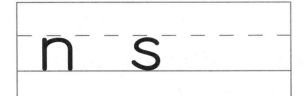 a and o!

Say the word the picture shows.

Write the missing letters to finish the word.

| n | | s | |

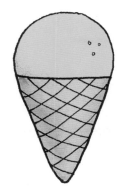

| c | | n | |

| c | | n | |

| r | | k | |

One Hungry Mule

Help the mule get to the fruit. Follow the path of long **u** words.

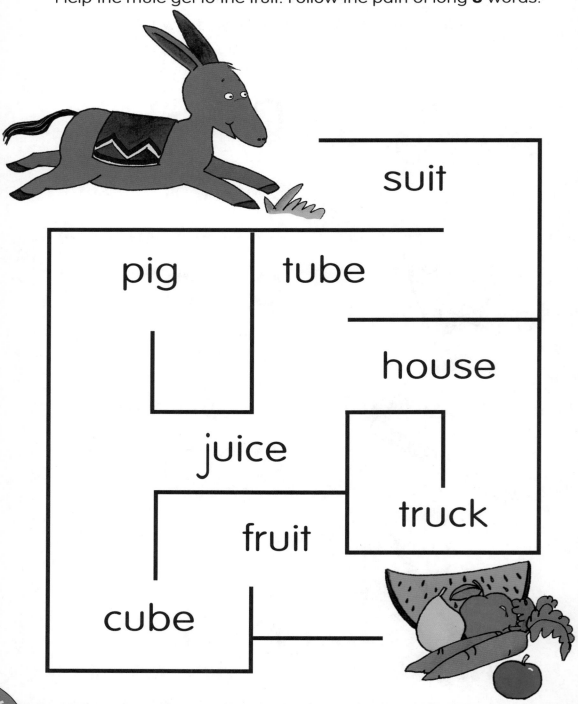

suit

pig

tube

house

juice

truck

fruit

cube

So Long, Vowels

Say the word the picture shows.

Write the missing letters to finish the word.

 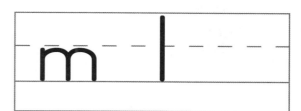

m l __ __

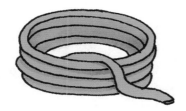 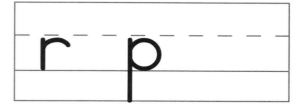

r __ p

 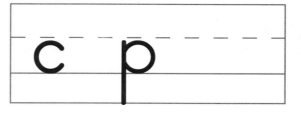

c __ p

 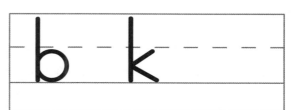

b __ k

Who Gets the e?

Look at each picture. Write an **e** at the end of
the word that has a long vowel sound.

man

man

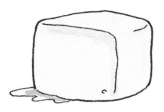

cub

cub

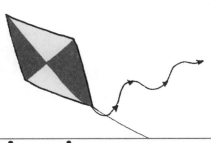
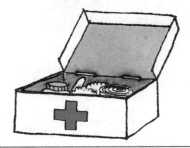

kit

kit

Give Me an oa?
Or Just an a?

Look at the pictures. Read the list of words.

Fill in the sentences with the missing words.

cat   coat   cot   boat   bat

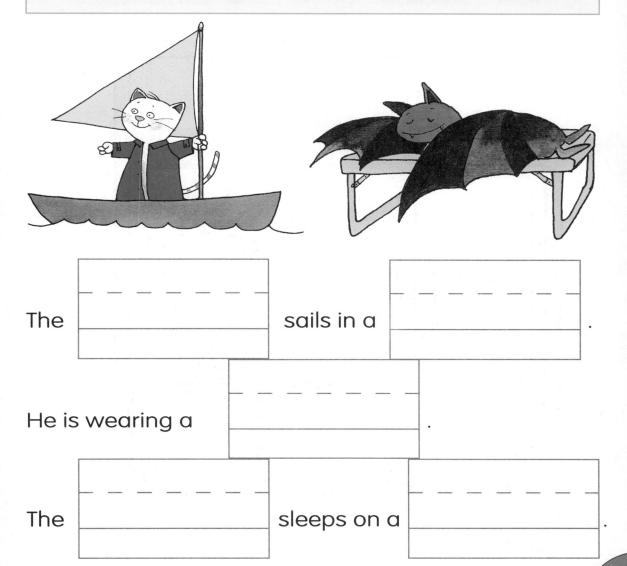

The _____ sails in a _____.

He is wearing a _____.

The _____ sleeps on a _____.

Hungry for Vowels

Draw a line from each word in the box to its picture.
Then color the foods that have a short vowel sound yellow,
and color the foods that have a long vowel sound green.

ham   fish   bun   cake   peas   fruit

Vowel Zoo

Each animal needs a friend.

Draw a line between animals with the same vowel sound.

fox

cat

seal

pig

bat

deer

fish

dog

Picking Up the Toys

Draw a line between each toy and the toy chest where it belongs.

doll

kite

book

Long Vowel Words

Short Vowel Words

bike

ball

boat

truck

Vowel Crossword

Use the picture clues to fill in the crossword puzzle.

| net | kite | tail | pane | tape |

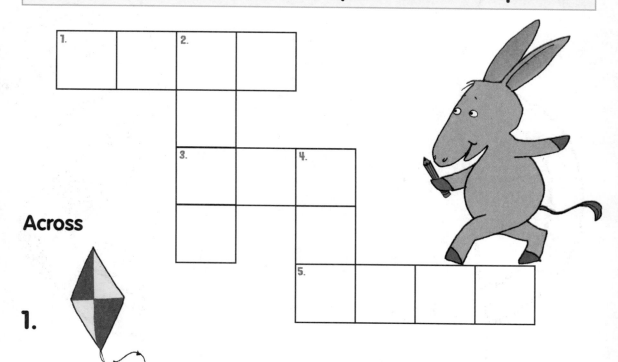

Across

1.

3.

5.

Down

2.

4.

AWESOME!

SUPER!

Great Job!

FlashKids
LEARNING IN A FLASH